Copyright © 2020 by Thandee & Jaymee

Presented to:

_____

_____

Thanks for being Awesome in so many Ways

ALWAYS DELIVER QUALITY

_____

_____
_____

_____
_____

_____
_____

_____
_____

_____
_____

_____
_____

_____
_____

_____
_____

_____
_____

TODAY I'M GRATEFUL FOR

Appreciate the moment

TODAY I'M GRATEFUL FOR

AUDIT YOUR MISTAKES

_____

_____

_____

_____

_____

_____

_____

_____

_____

_____

_____

_____

_____

TODAY I'M GRATEFUL FOR

BE A GIVER

_____

_____

_____

_____

_____

_____

_____

_____

_____

_____

_____

_____

_____

_____

TODAY I'M GRATEFUL FOR

BE A GOAL GETTER!

_____

_____

_____

_____

_____

_____

_____

_____

_____

_____

_____

_____

_____

TODAY I'M GRATEFUL FOR

Be constantly curious

TODAY I'M GRATEFUL FOR

BE THE CHANGE

_____

_____

_____

_____

_____

_____

_____

_____

_____

_____

_____

_____

_____

_____

TODAY I'M GRATEFUL FOR

Be the best version of you!

_____

_____

_____

_____

_____

_____

_____

_____

_____

_____

_____

_____

_____

_____

_____

TODAY I'M GRATEFUL FOR

Be obsessively grateful

_____

_____

_____

_____

_____

_____

_____

_____

_____

_____

_____

_____

_____

_____

TODAY I'M GRATEFUL FOR

BELIEVE YOU CAN

TODAY I'M GRATEFUL FOR

BLOCK OUT HATERS

TODAY I'M GRATEFUL FOR

Brainstorm alternative ideas

TODAY I'M GRATEFUL FOR

Branding is essential

_____

_____

_____

_____

_____

_____

_____

_____

_____

_____

_____

_____

_____

TODAY I'M GRATEFUL FOR

BUILD QUALITY RELATIONSHIPS

TODAY I'M GRATEFUL FOR

Build strategic partnerships

CELEBRATE ALL SUCCESS

TODAY I'M GRATEFUL FOR

COMPETITION FUELS GROWTH

_____

_____

_____

_____

_____

_____

_____

_____

_____

_____

_____

_____

_____

TODAY I'M GRATEFUL FOR

COUNT YOUR BLESSINGS

TODAY I'M GRATEFUL FOR

DARE TO SUCK

TODAY I'M GRATEFUL FOR

DO IT NOW

TODAY I'M GRATEFUL FOR

Embrace constant change

_____

_____

_____

_____

_____

_____

_____

_____

_____

_____

_____

_____

_____

_____

TODAY I'M GRATEFUL FOR

ENJOY LIFE

TODAY I'M GRATEFUL FOR

EVERY MOMENT MATTERS

TODAY I'M GRATEFUL FOR

Exceptional makes memorable

FEED YOUR SOUL

_____

_____

_____

_____

_____

_____

_____

_____

_____

_____

_____

_____

_____

TODAY I'M GRATEFUL FOR

Focus and win

TODAY I'M GRATEFUL FOR

Good vibes only

TODAY I'M GRATEFUL FOR

TODAY I'M GRATEFUL FOR

Handle breakdowns immediately

Happiness is Choice

TODAY I'M GRATEFUL FOR

HEALTH IS WEALTH

_____

_____

_____

_____

_____

_____

_____

_____

_____

_____

_____

_____

_____

_____

TODAY I'M GRATEFUL FOR

Identify key milestones

_____

_____

_____

_____

_____

_____

_____

_____

_____

_____

_____

_____

_____

_____

_____

_____

_____

TODAY I'M GRATEFUL FOR

It is possible

_____

_____

_____

_____

_____

_____

_____

_____

_____

_____

_____

_____

_____

_____

TODAY I'M GRATEFUL FOR

Keep moving forward

TODAY I'M GRATEFUL FOR

KEEP MORALE HIGH

TODAY I'M GRATEFUL FOR

LAUGHTER IS MEDICINE

TODAY I'M GRATEFUL FOR

Leaders are early

_____

_____

_____

_____

_____

_____

_____

_____

_____

_____

_____

_____

_____

_____

TODAY I'M GRATEFUL FOR

LEARN FROM YESTERDAY

TODAY I'M GRATEFUL FOR

Life is awesome

TODAY I'M GRATEFUL FOR

Life won't wait

TODAY I'M GRATEFUL FOR

Live life daily

TODAY I'M GRATEFUL FOR

LIVE, LOVE, LAUGH

TODAY I'M GRATEFUL FOR

LIVE YOUR POTENTIAL

TODAY I'M GRATEFUL FOR

MAINTAIN YOUR INTEGRITY

TODAY I'M GRATEFUL FOR

MANAGE YOUR REPUTATION

_____

_____

_____

_____

_____

_____

_____

_____

_____

_____

_____

_____

_____

_____

TODAY I'M GRATEFUL FOR

MANAGE RESOURCES EFFECTIVELY

_____

_____

_____

_____

_____

_____

_____

_____

_____

_____

_____

_____

_____

_____

_____

_____

_____

_____

TODAY I'M GRATEFUL FOR

Mastery abhors mediocrity

_____

_____
_____

_____

_____

_____

_____

_____

_____

_____

_____

_____

_____

_____

_____

TODAY I'M GRATEFUL FOR

MODEL THE MASTERS

TODAY I'M GRATEFUL FOR

MONITOR BUDGETS REGULARLY

TODAY I'M GRATEFUL FOR

NEVER GIVE UP

_____

_____

_____

_____

_____

_____

_____

_____

_____

_____

_____

_____

_____

_____

TODAY I'M GRATEFUL FOR

TODAY I'M GRATEFUL FOR

Nothing is Impossible

TODAY I'M GRATEFUL FOR

NOW OR NEVER

TODAY I'M GRATEFUL FOR

Nurture your best

TODAY I'M GRATEFUL FOR

Peace, love & happiness

_____

_____

_____

_____

_____

_____

_____

_____

_____

_____

_____

_____

_____

_____

_____

_____

TODAY I'M GRATEFUL FOR

Perfectionism stalls progress

TODAY I'M GRATEFUL FOR

PRIORITIZE ALL TASKS

TODAY I'M GRATEFUL FOR

REDUCE YOUR OVERHEADS

TODAY I'M GRATEFUL FOR

Remember to Live

TODAY I'M GRATEFUL FOR

Reward high performance

TODAY I'M GRATEFUL FOR

Seize the day

_____

_____

_____

_____

_____

_____

_____

_____

_____

_____

_____

_____

_____

_____

TODAY I'M GRATEFUL FOR

Set clear targets

_____

_____

_____

_____

_____

_____

_____

_____

_____

_____

_____

_____

_____

TODAY I'M GRATEFUL FOR

Settle your debts

TODAY I'M GRATEFUL FOR

Speak the truth

_____

TODAY I'M GRATEFUL FOR

Stop underestimating yourself

TODAY I'M GRATEFUL FOR

Success breeds success

_____

_____

_____

_____

_____

_____

_____

_____

_____

_____

_____

_____

_____

_____

_____

TODAY I'M GRATEFUL FOR

SUCCESS IS YOURS

TODAY I'M GRATEFUL FOR

TAKE THE RISK

TODAY I'M GRATEFUL FOR

Teamwork makes the dream work

TODAY I'M GRATEFUL FOR

TIME HEALS EVERYTHING

_____

_____

_____

_____

_____

_____

_____

_____

_____

_____

_____

_____

_____

TODAY I'M GRATEFUL FOR

THINK OUTSIDE THE BOX

TODAY I'M GRATEFUL FOR

Track all progress

TODAY I'M GRATEFUL FOR

Value Your Time

WINNERS NEVER QUIT

TODAY I'M GRATEFUL FOR

Yes, you can!

_____

_____

_____

_____

_____

_____

_____

_____

_____

_____

_____

_____

_____

TODAY I'M GRATEFUL FOR

You're awesome and I know it!

TODAY I'M GRATEFUL FOR

YOU'VE GOT THIS!

TODAY I'M GRATEFUL FOR

Never have a lack of goals.

"If you're bored with life, you don't get up every morning with a burning desire to do things – you don't have enough goals."

—LOU HOLTZ

Key Objective _____

Goal Checklist

_____ ☐
_____ ☐
_____ ☐
_____ ☐
_____ ☐
_____ ☐
_____ ☐
_____ ☐
_____ ☐
_____ ☐

Places to Visit

_____ ☐
_____ ☐
_____ ☐
_____ ☐
_____ ☐

People to Meet

_____ ☐
_____ ☐
_____ ☐
_____ ☐
_____ ☐

Notes

Key Objective ⭐

Goal Checklist

☐
☐
☐
☐
☐
☐
☐
☐
☐
☐

Places to Visit

☐
☐
☐
☐
☐

People to Meet

☐
☐
☐
☐
☐

Notes

Key Objective _____ ★

Goal Checklist

☐
☐
☐
☐
☐
☐
☐
☐
☐
☐

Places to Visit ☐
☐
☐
☐
☐

People to Meet ☐
☐
☐
☐
☐

Notes

Key Objective _____ ⭐

Goal Checklist

	☐
	☐
	☐
	☐
	☐
	☐
	☐
	☐
	☐
	☐

Places to Visit

	☐
	☐
	☐
	☐
	☐

People to Meet

	☐
	☐
	☐
	☐
	☐

Notes

Key Objective _____ ★

Goal Checklist

☐
_____
☐
_____
☐
_____
☐
_____
☐
_____
☐
_____
☐
_____
☐
_____
☐
_____
☐

Places to Visit

☐
_____
☐
_____
☐
_____
☐
_____
☐

People to Meet

☐
_____
☐
_____
☐
_____
☐
_____
☐

Notes

Key Objective _____ ⭐

Goal Checklist

_____ ☐
_____ ☐
_____ ☐
_____ ☐
_____ ☐
_____ ☐
_____ ☐
_____ ☐
_____ ☐
_____ ☐

Places to Visit

_____ ☐
_____ ☐
_____ ☐
_____ ☐
_____ ☐

People to Meet

_____ ☐
_____ ☐
_____ ☐
_____ ☐
_____ ☐

Notes

Key Objective

Goal Checklist

Places to Visit

People to Meet

Notes

Key Objective _____ ⭐

Goal Checklist

_____ ☐
_____ ☐
_____ ☐
_____ ☐
_____ ☐
_____ ☐
_____ ☐
_____ ☐
_____ ☐
_____ ☐

Places to Visit

_____ ☐
_____ ☐
_____ ☐
_____ ☐
_____ ☐

People to Meet

_____ ☐
_____ ☐
_____ ☐
_____ ☐
_____ ☐

Notes

Key Objective _____ ⭐

Goal Checklist

_____ ☐
_____ ☐
_____ ☐
_____ ☐
_____ ☐
_____ ☐
_____ ☐
_____ ☐
_____ ☐
_____ ☐

Places to Visit

_____ ☐
_____ ☐
_____ ☐
_____ ☐
_____ ☐

People to Meet

_____ ☐
_____ ☐
_____ ☐
_____ ☐
_____ ☐

Notes

Weekly Checklist

Monday

- [ ] _____
- [ ] _____
- [ ] _____
- [ ] _____
- [ ] _____

Tuesday

- [ ] _____
- [ ] _____
- [ ] _____
- [ ] _____
- [ ] _____

Wednesday

- [ ] _____
- [ ] _____
- [ ] _____
- [ ] _____
- [ ] _____

Thursday

- [ ] _____
- [ ] _____
- [ ] _____
- [ ] _____
- [ ] _____

Friday

- [ ] _____
- [ ] _____
- [ ] _____
- [ ] _____
- [ ] _____

Saturday

- [ ] _____
- [ ] _____
- [ ] _____
- [ ] _____
- [ ] _____

Sunday

- [ ] _____
- [ ] _____
- [ ] _____
- [ ] _____
- [ ] _____

Every Day

- [ ] _____
- [ ] _____
- [ ] _____
- [ ] _____
- [ ] _____

Weekly Checklist

Monday

_____ ☐
_____ ☐
_____ ☐
_____ ☐
_____ ☐

Tuesday

_____ ☐
_____ ☐
_____ ☐
_____ ☐
_____ ☐

Wednesday

_____ ☐
_____ ☐
_____ ☐
_____ ☐
_____ ☐

Thursday

_____ ☐
_____ ☐
_____ ☐
_____ ☐
_____ ☐

Friday

_____ ☐
_____ ☐
_____ ☐
_____ ☐
_____ ☐

Saturday

_____ ☐
_____ ☐
_____ ☐
_____ ☐
_____ ☐

Sunday

_____ ☐
_____ ☐
_____ ☐
_____ ☐
_____ ☐

Every Day

_____ ☐
_____ ☐
_____ ☐
_____ ☐
_____ ☐

Weekly Checklist

Monday

- [ ] _____
- [ ] _____
- [ ] _____
- [ ] _____
- [ ] _____

Tuesday

- [ ] _____
- [ ] _____
- [ ] _____
- [ ] _____
- [ ] _____

Wednesday

- [ ] _____
- [ ] _____
- [ ] _____
- [ ] _____
- [ ] _____

Thursday

- [ ] _____
- [ ] _____
- [ ] _____
- [ ] _____
- [ ] _____

Friday

- [ ] _____
- [ ] _____
- [ ] _____
- [ ] _____
- [ ] _____

Saturday

- [ ] _____
- [ ] _____
- [ ] _____
- [ ] _____
- [ ] _____

Sunday

- [ ] _____
- [ ] _____
- [ ] _____
- [ ] _____
- [ ] _____

Every Day

- [ ] _____
- [ ] _____
- [ ] _____
- [ ] _____
- [ ] _____

Weekly Checklist

Monday

- [ ] _____
- [ ] _____
- [ ] _____
- [ ] _____
- [ ] _____

Tuesday

- [ ] _____
- [ ] _____
- [ ] _____
- [ ] _____
- [ ] _____

Wednesday

- [ ] _____
- [ ] _____
- [ ] _____
- [ ] _____
- [ ] _____

Thursday

- [ ] _____
- [ ] _____
- [ ] _____
- [ ] _____
- [ ] _____

Friday

- [ ] _____
- [ ] _____
- [ ] _____
- [ ] _____
- [ ] _____

Saturday

- [ ] _____
- [ ] _____
- [ ] _____
- [ ] _____
- [ ] _____

Sunday

- [ ] _____
- [ ] _____
- [ ] _____
- [ ] _____
- [ ] _____

Every Day

- [ ] _____
- [ ] _____
- [ ] _____
- [ ] _____
- [ ] _____

Weekly Checklist

Monday

- _____ ☐
- _____ ☐
- _____ ☐
- _____ ☐
- _____ ☐

Tuesday

- _____ ☐
- _____ ☐
- _____ ☐
- _____ ☐
- _____ ☐

Wednesday

- _____ ☐
- _____ ☐
- _____ ☐
- _____ ☐
- _____ ☐

Thursday

- _____ ☐
- _____ ☐
- _____ ☐
- _____ ☐
- _____ ☐

Friday

- _____ ☐
- _____ ☐
- _____ ☐
- _____ ☐
- _____ ☐

Saturday

- _____ ☐
- _____ ☐
- _____ ☐
- _____ ☐
- _____ ☐

Sunday

- _____ ☐
- _____ ☐
- _____ ☐
- _____ ☐
- _____ ☐

Every Day

- _____ ☐
- _____ ☐
- _____ ☐
- _____ ☐
- _____ ☐

Weekly Checklist

Monday

- _____ ☐
- _____ ☐
- _____ ☐
- _____ ☐
- _____ ☐

Tuesday

- _____ ☐
- _____ ☐
- _____ ☐
- _____ ☐
- _____ ☐

Wednesday

- _____ ☐
- _____ ☐
- _____ ☐
- _____ ☐
- _____ ☐

Thursday

- _____ ☐
- _____ ☐
- _____ ☐
- _____ ☐
- _____ ☐

Friday

- _____ ☐
- _____ ☐
- _____ ☐
- _____ ☐
- _____ ☐

Saturday

- _____ ☐
- _____ ☐
- _____ ☐
- _____ ☐
- _____ ☐

Sunday

- _____ ☐
- _____ ☐
- _____ ☐
- _____ ☐
- _____ ☐

Every Day

- _____ ☐
- _____ ☐
- _____ ☐
- _____ ☐
- _____ ☐

Weekly Checklist

Monday

- _____ ☐
- _____ ☐
- _____ ☐
- _____ ☐
- _____ ☐

Tuesday

- _____ ☐
- _____ ☐
- _____ ☐
- _____ ☐
- _____ ☐

Wednesday

- _____ ☐
- _____ ☐
- _____ ☐
- _____ ☐
- _____ ☐

Thursday

- _____ ☐
- _____ ☐
- _____ ☐
- _____ ☐
- _____ ☐

Friday

- _____ ☐
- _____ ☐
- _____ ☐
- _____ ☐
- _____ ☐

Saturday

- _____ ☐
- _____ ☐
- _____ ☐
- _____ ☐
- _____ ☐

Sunday

- _____ ☐
- _____ ☐
- _____ ☐
- _____ ☐
- _____ ☐

Every Day

- _____ ☐
- _____ ☐
- _____ ☐
- _____ ☐
- _____ ☐

Weekly Checklist

Monday

- [ ]
- [ ]
- [ ]
- [ ]
- [ ]

Tuesday

- [ ]
- [ ]
- [ ]
- [ ]
- [ ]

Wednesday

- [ ]
- [ ]
- [ ]
- [ ]
- [ ]

Thursday

- [ ]
- [ ]
- [ ]
- [ ]
- [ ]

Friday

- [ ]
- [ ]
- [ ]
- [ ]
- [ ]

Saturday

- [ ]
- [ ]
- [ ]
- [ ]
- [ ]

Sunday

- [ ]
- [ ]
- [ ]
- [ ]
- [ ]

Every Day

- [ ]
- [ ]
- [ ]
- [ ]
- [ ]

Weekly Checklist

Monday

- .... ☐
- .... ☐
- .... ☐
- .... ☐
- .... ☐

Tuesday

- .... ☐
- .... ☐
- .... ☐
- .... ☐
- .... ☐

Wednesday

- .... ☐
- .... ☐
- .... ☐
- .... ☐
- .... ☐

Thursday

- .... ☐
- .... ☐
- .... ☐
- .... ☐
- .... ☐

Friday

- .... ☐
- .... ☐
- .... ☐
- .... ☐
- .... ☐

Saturday

- .... ☐
- .... ☐
- .... ☐
- .... ☐
- .... ☐

Sunday

- .... ☐
- .... ☐
- .... ☐
- .... ☐
- .... ☐

Every Day

- .... ☐
- .... ☐
- .... ☐
- .... ☐
- .... ☐

Weekly Checklist

Monday

- _____ ☐
- _____ ☐
- _____ ☐
- _____ ☐
- _____ ☐

Tuesday

- _____ ☐
- _____ ☐
- _____ ☐
- _____ ☐
- _____ ☐

Wednesday

- _____ ☐
- _____ ☐
- _____ ☐
- _____ ☐
- _____ ☐

Thursday

- _____ ☐
- _____ ☐
- _____ ☐
- _____ ☐
- _____ ☐

Friday

- _____ ☐
- _____ ☐
- _____ ☐
- _____ ☐
- _____ ☐

Saturday

- _____ ☐
- _____ ☐
- _____ ☐
- _____ ☐
- _____ ☐

Sunday

- _____ ☐
- _____ ☐
- _____ ☐
- _____ ☐
- _____ ☐

Every Day

- _____ ☐
- _____ ☐
- _____ ☐
- _____ ☐
- _____ ☐

Weekly Checklist

Monday

- [ ] _____
- [ ] _____
- [ ] _____
- [ ] _____
- [ ] _____

Tuesday

- [ ] _____
- [ ] _____
- [ ] _____
- [ ] _____
- [ ] _____

Wednesday

- [ ] _____
- [ ] _____
- [ ] _____
- [ ] _____
- [ ] _____

Thursday

- [ ] _____
- [ ] _____
- [ ] _____
- [ ] _____
- [ ] _____

Friday

- [ ] _____
- [ ] _____
- [ ] _____
- [ ] _____
- [ ] _____

Saturday

- [ ] _____
- [ ] _____
- [ ] _____
- [ ] _____
- [ ] _____

Sunday

- [ ] _____
- [ ] _____
- [ ] _____
- [ ] _____
- [ ] _____

Every Day

- [ ] _____
- [ ] _____
- [ ] _____
- [ ] _____
- [ ] _____

Weekly Checklist

Monday

- [ ] _____
- [ ] _____
- [ ] _____
- [ ] _____
- [ ] _____

Tuesday

- [ ] _____
- [ ] _____
- [ ] _____
- [ ] _____
- [ ] _____

Wednesday

- [ ] _____
- [ ] _____
- [ ] _____
- [ ] _____
- [ ] _____

Thursday

- [ ] _____
- [ ] _____
- [ ] _____
- [ ] _____
- [ ] _____

Friday

- [ ] _____
- [ ] _____
- [ ] _____
- [ ] _____
- [ ] _____

Saturday

- [ ] _____
- [ ] _____
- [ ] _____
- [ ] _____
- [ ] _____

Sunday

- [ ] _____
- [ ] _____
- [ ] _____
- [ ] _____
- [ ] _____

Every Day

- [ ] _____
- [ ] _____
- [ ] _____
- [ ] _____
- [ ] _____

Weekly Checklist

Monday

- _____ ☐
- _____ ☐
- _____ ☐
- _____ ☐
- _____ ☐

Tuesday

- _____ ☐
- _____ ☐
- _____ ☐
- _____ ☐
- _____ ☐

Wednesday

- _____ ☐
- _____ ☐
- _____ ☐
- _____ ☐
- _____ ☐

Thursday

- _____ ☐
- _____ ☐
- _____ ☐
- _____ ☐
- _____ ☐

Friday

- _____ ☐
- _____ ☐
- _____ ☐
- _____ ☐
- _____ ☐

Saturday

- _____ ☐
- _____ ☐
- _____ ☐
- _____ ☐
- _____ ☐

Sunday

- _____ ☐
- _____ ☐
- _____ ☐
- _____ ☐
- _____ ☐

Every Day

- _____ ☐
- _____ ☐
- _____ ☐
- _____ ☐
- _____ ☐

Weekly Checklist

Monday

- [ ] _____
- [ ] _____
- [ ] _____
- [ ] _____
- [ ] _____

Tuesday

- [ ] _____
- [ ] _____
- [ ] _____
- [ ] _____
- [ ] _____

Wednesday

- [ ] _____
- [ ] _____
- [ ] _____
- [ ] _____
- [ ] _____

Thursday

- [ ] _____
- [ ] _____
- [ ] _____
- [ ] _____
- [ ] _____

Friday

- [ ] _____
- [ ] _____
- [ ] _____
- [ ] _____
- [ ] _____

Saturday

- [ ] _____
- [ ] _____
- [ ] _____
- [ ] _____
- [ ] _____

Sunday

- [ ] _____
- [ ] _____
- [ ] _____
- [ ] _____
- [ ] _____

Every Day

- [ ] _____
- [ ] _____
- [ ] _____
- [ ] _____
- [ ] _____

Weekly Checklist

Monday

- [ ] _____
- [ ] _____
- [ ] _____
- [ ] _____
- [ ] _____

Tuesday

- [ ] _____
- [ ] _____
- [ ] _____
- [ ] _____
- [ ] _____

Wednesday

- [ ] _____
- [ ] _____
- [ ] _____
- [ ] _____
- [ ] _____

Thursday

- [ ] _____
- [ ] _____
- [ ] _____
- [ ] _____
- [ ] _____

Friday

- [ ] _____
- [ ] _____
- [ ] _____
- [ ] _____
- [ ] _____

Saturday

- [ ] _____
- [ ] _____
- [ ] _____
- [ ] _____
- [ ] _____

Sunday

- [ ] _____
- [ ] _____
- [ ] _____
- [ ] _____
- [ ] _____

Every Day

- [ ] _____
- [ ] _____
- [ ] _____
- [ ] _____
- [ ] _____

Weekly Checklist

Monday

- _____ ☐
- _____ ☐
- _____ ☐
- _____ ☐
- _____ ☐

Tuesday

- _____ ☐
- _____ ☐
- _____ ☐
- _____ ☐
- _____ ☐

Wednesday

- _____ ☐
- _____ ☐
- _____ ☐
- _____ ☐
- _____ ☐

Thursday

- _____ ☐
- _____ ☐
- _____ ☐
- _____ ☐
- _____ ☐

Friday

- _____ ☐
- _____ ☐
- _____ ☐
- _____ ☐
- _____ ☐

Saturday

- _____ ☐
- _____ ☐
- _____ ☐
- _____ ☐
- _____ ☐

Sunday

- _____ ☐
- _____ ☐
- _____ ☐
- _____ ☐
- _____ ☐

Every Day

- _____ ☐
- _____ ☐
- _____ ☐
- _____ ☐
- _____ ☐

Weekly Checklist

Monday

- _____ ☐
- _____ ☐
- _____ ☐
- _____ ☐
- _____ ☐

Tuesday

- _____ ☐
- _____ ☐
- _____ ☐
- _____ ☐
- _____ ☐

Wednesday

- _____ ☐
- _____ ☐
- _____ ☐
- _____ ☐
- _____ ☐

Thursday

- _____ ☐
- _____ ☐
- _____ ☐
- _____ ☐
- _____ ☐

Friday

- _____ ☐
- _____ ☐
- _____ ☐
- _____ ☐
- _____ ☐

Saturday

- _____ ☐
- _____ ☐
- _____ ☐
- _____ ☐
- _____ ☐

Sunday

- _____ ☐
- _____ ☐
- _____ ☐
- _____ ☐
- _____ ☐

Every Day

- _____ ☐
- _____ ☐
- _____ ☐
- _____ ☐
- _____ ☐

Weekly Checklist

Monday

- [ ] _____
- [ ] _____
- [ ] _____
- [ ] _____
- [ ] _____

Tuesday

- [ ] _____
- [ ] _____
- [ ] _____
- [ ] _____
- [ ] _____

Wednesday

- [ ] _____
- [ ] _____
- [ ] _____
- [ ] _____
- [ ] _____

Thursday

- [ ] _____
- [ ] _____
- [ ] _____
- [ ] _____
- [ ] _____

Friday

- [ ] _____
- [ ] _____
- [ ] _____
- [ ] _____
- [ ] _____

Saturday

- [ ] _____
- [ ] _____
- [ ] _____
- [ ] _____
- [ ] _____

Sunday

- [ ] _____
- [ ] _____
- [ ] _____
- [ ] _____
- [ ] _____

Every Day

- [ ] _____
- [ ] _____
- [ ] _____
- [ ] _____
- [ ] _____

Weekly Checklist

Monday

- _____ ☐
- _____ ☐
- _____ ☐
- _____ ☐
- _____ ☐

Tuesday

- _____ ☐
- _____ ☐
- _____ ☐
- _____ ☐
- _____ ☐

Wednesday

- _____ ☐
- _____ ☐
- _____ ☐
- _____ ☐
- _____ ☐

Thursday

- _____ ☐
- _____ ☐
- _____ ☐
- _____ ☐
- _____ ☐

Friday

- _____ ☐
- _____ ☐
- _____ ☐
- _____ ☐
- _____ ☐

Saturday

- _____ ☐
- _____ ☐
- _____ ☐
- _____ ☐
- _____ ☐

Sunday

- _____ ☐
- _____ ☐
- _____ ☐
- _____ ☐
- _____ ☐

Every Day

- _____ ☐
- _____ ☐
- _____ ☐
- _____ ☐
- _____ ☐

Weekly Checklist

Monday

- [ ] _____
- [ ] _____
- [ ] _____
- [ ] _____
- [ ] _____

Tuesday

- [ ] _____
- [ ] _____
- [ ] _____
- [ ] _____
- [ ] _____

Wednesday

- [ ] _____
- [ ] _____
- [ ] _____
- [ ] _____
- [ ] _____

Thursday

- [ ] _____
- [ ] _____
- [ ] _____
- [ ] _____
- [ ] _____

Friday

- [ ] _____
- [ ] _____
- [ ] _____
- [ ] _____
- [ ] _____

Saturday

- [ ] _____
- [ ] _____
- [ ] _____
- [ ] _____
- [ ] _____

Sunday

- [ ] _____
- [ ] _____
- [ ] _____
- [ ] _____
- [ ] _____

Every Day

- [ ] _____
- [ ] _____
- [ ] _____
- [ ] _____
- [ ] _____

Printed in Great Britain
by Amazon

15200143R00063

Thandee ♥ Jaymee

ISBN 9798569097487
9 798569 097487